Grammar Friends 1

Tim Ward

OXFORD
UNIVERSITY PRESS

OXFORD
UNIVERSITY PRESS

Great Clarendon Street, Oxford OX2 6DP

Oxford University Press is a department of the University of Oxford.
It furthers the University's objective of excellence in research, scholarship,
and education by publishing worldwide in

Oxford New York

Auckland Cape Town Dar es Salaam Hong Kong Karachi
Kuala Lumpur Madrid Melbourne Mexico City Nairobi
New Delhi Shanghai Taipei Toronto

With offices in

Argentina Austria Brazil Chile Czech Republic France Greece
Guatemala Hungary Italy Japan Poland Portugal Singapore
South Korea Switzerland Thailand Turkey Ukraine Vietnam

OXFORD and OXFORD ENGLISH are registered trade marks of
Oxford University Press in the UK and in certain other countries

© Oxford University Press 2009

The moral rights of the author have been asserted

Database right Oxford University Press (maker)

First published 2009
2023
26

No unauthorized photocopying

All rights reserved. No part of this publication may be reproduced,
stored in a retrieval system, or transmitted, in any form or by any means,
without the prior permission in writing of Oxford University Press,
or as expressly permitted by law, or under terms agreed with the appropriate
reprographics rights organization. Enquiries concerning reproduction
outside the scope of the above should be sent to the ELT Rights Department,
Oxford University Press, at the address above

You must not circulate this book in any other binding or cover
and you must impose this same condition on any acquirer

Any websites referred to in this publication are in the public domain and
their addresses are provided by Oxford University Press for information only.
Oxford University Press disclaims any responsibility for the content

ISBN: 978 0 19 478000 1

Printed in China

This book is printed on paper from certified and well-managed sources.

ACKNOWLEDGEMENTS

Illustrations by: Andy Keylock/Beehive Illustration (characters) and Simon Smith

Contents

Starter Hello!	Question words	**What ...? Who ...? How ...? How old ...?**	4
1 School things	Questions with **is** The indefinite article	**What's this?** **A** and **an**	8
2 My toys	Possessive adjectives (1) Present simple of **be** (1)	**My** and **your** **Is this ...? Yes, it is. No, it isn't.**	12
3 My body	Regular plural nouns Present simple of **be** (2) Demonstratives	Plural **–s** **Are** **This** and **these**	16
Review 1			20
4 Jobs	Subject pronouns (1) Yes/no questions (1)	**He** and **she** Questions with **is**	22
5 At the park	Wh- questions (1) Prepositions of place	**Where's ...?** **In**, **on** and **under**	26
6 My family	Subject pronouns (2) Yes/no questions (2) Possessive **'s**	**I'm** and **you're** **Are you ...?** Jamie**'s** and Alison**'s**	30
Review 2			34
7 Clothes	Yes/no questions (3) Possessive adjectives (2)	**Are they ...? Yes, they are. No, they aren't.** **His** and **her**	36
8 My home	Wh- questions (2) Yes/no questions (4) Adverbs	**Where are ...?** **Is he in ...? Is she in ...? Are they in ...?** **Upstairs** and **downstairs**	40
9 My lunch	**Have got** (1)	**I've got** and **I haven't got** **Have you got ...? Yes, I have. No, I haven't.**	44
Review 3			48
10 My friends	**Have got** (2)	**He's got, she's got** and **it's got**	50
11 Zoo trip	Present simple: **like** (1) Adjectives	**I like** and **I don't like** Adjectives	54
12 Family meal	Present simple: **like** (2) Wh- questions (3)	**Do you like ...?** **What do you like?**	58
Review 4			62
13 My room	**There's** and **there are**	**There's** and **there are** **Is there ...?** **Yes, there is. No, there isn't**	64
14 Abilities	**Can** for ability	**Can** and **can't** **Can it ...? Yes, it can. No, it can't.**	68
15 At the beach	**Let's** Imperatives Negative imperatives	**Let's ...** Imperatives Negative imperatives	72
Review 5			76
Grammar reference			78

Starter Hello!

Question words

What ...? Who ...? How ...?

In a question, **what** asks about things and **who** asks about people.
We say **How are you?** when we meet someone.

1 Match.

1 Hello.
2 What's your name?
3 How are you?
4 Who's this?

I'm fine, thank you.
This is Alison.
My name's Jamie.
Hello.

2 Look and write.

~~Hello~~   What's   How   Who's

How old ...?

3 Match.

1 How old are you?      I'm two.

2 How old are you?      I'm three.

3 How old are you?      I'm six.

4 How old are you?      I'm five.

5 How old are you?      I'm four.

4 Write.

~~four~~ ~~seven~~ ~~you~~   you   three   are you   old are you   eight   ten

1 How old are you?   I'm _seven_ .

2 How old are _you_ ?   I'm _____ .

3 How old are _____ ?   I'm _____ .

4 How old _____ ?   I'm _____ .

5 How _____ ?   I'm _____ .

5 Read and colour. Find the hidden word.

Colour **what** red.   Colour **who** blue.   Colour **how** yellow.

what	how	how	how	how	how	how	how	what	how	who	how	how	how	how
what	how	how	how	how	how	how	how	what	how	who	how	how	how	how
what	how	how	how	how	how	how	how	what	how	who	how	how	how	how
what	what	what	how	who	who	who	how	what	how	who	how	what	what	what
what	how	what	how	who	how	who	how	what	how	who	how	what	how	what
what	how	what	how	who	who	who	how	what	how	who	how	what	how	what
what	how	what	how	how	how	how	how	what	how	who	how	what	how	what
what	how	what	how	who	who	who	how	what	how	who	how	what	what	what

1 School things

Questions with *is*
The indefinite article

What's this?

 **What's this?** is a question. We use it to find out about things. We can answer with **It's a** ...

1 Write and match.

1 What's this? — It's a pencil.

2 What's _____ ? _____ door.

3 _____ this? _____ window.

4 _____ ? _____ book.

A and an

 **A** and **an** are articles. They come before singular nouns.
It's **a** pencil.
It's **a** book.

We use **an** before **a, e, i, o** or **u**.
It's **an** apple.

8   Unit 1

2 Write the words in the correct box.

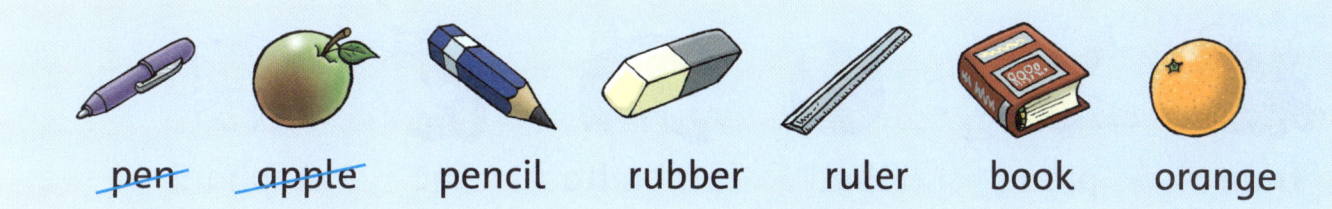

~~pen~~   ~~apple~~   pencil   rubber   ruler   book   orange

a

pen
_____
_____
_____
_____

an

apple
_____
_____
_____
_____

3 Write **a** or **an**.

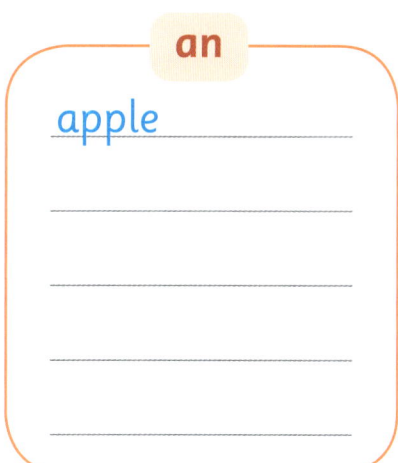

1 What's this?   It's __a__ bag.

2 And what's this?   It's _____ orange.

3 What's this?   It's _____ book.

4 What's this?   It's _____ apple.

5 And what's this?   It's _____ pencil case.

Unit 1

4 Write. Remember a or an.

train   plane   ~~ball~~   umbrella   cat   elephant

1 What's this?   It's _a ball_.

2 What's _this_ ?   It's _____.

3 What's _____?   It's _____.

4 _____?   _____.

5 _____?   _____.

6 _____?   _____.

5 **What's this? Draw and write.**

apple   book   orange   train   ~~ball~~   elephant

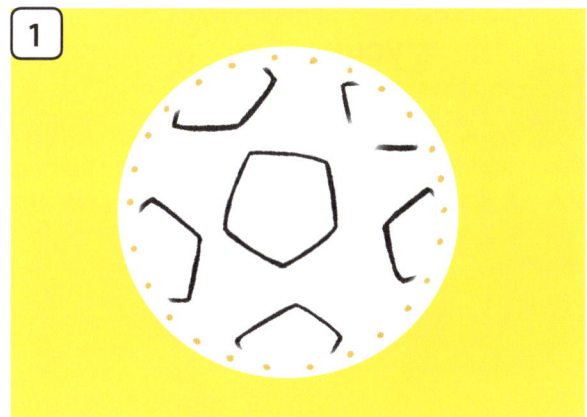

It's a ball. _____.

_____. _____.

_____. _____.

2 My toys

Possessive adjectives (1)
Present simple of *be* (1)

My and your

My and **your** are possessive adjectives. They say who owns something.
I   **my** train, **my** ball, **my** car
you   **your** car, **your** train, **your** teddy

1 Match.

2 Circle **my** and **your**.

3 Write **my** or **your**.

1 This is __my__ ball.
2 This is _____ teddy.
3 This is _____ car.
4 This is _____ kite.
5 This is _____ train.

4 Write **my** or **your** and complete the words.

1 This is __your__ t__rain__.
2 This is _____ te_____.
3 This is _____ c_____.
4 This is _____ k_____.
5 This is _____ b_____.

Unit 2

Is this ...? Yes, it is. No, it isn't.

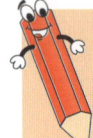 We use **is** to identify someone or something. **Is** comes from the verb **be**.

 This **is** Alison.    This **is** my car.

Is this ...? is a yes/no question. We change the word order in questions.

Statement   Question
This is your teddy.   *Is this* your teddy?

Yes, it is and **No, it isn't** are short answers. We can use them if the question begins with **Is this ...?**
Is this your car?   Yes, it is.   No, it isn't.

isn't = is not

5 Match.

1  Is this a car?   2 Is this a ball?

                        Yes, it is.

3  Is this a kite?   4  Is this a train?

                        No, it isn't.

5  Is this a book?   6  Is this a doll?

14 Unit 2

6 Write the words in the correct order. Make questions.

1 this your ball Is

   Is this your ball ?

2 my doll Is this

   Is this my doll ?

3 my this Is car

   _____ ?

4 Is kite this your

   _____ ?

5 puzzle your this Is

   _____ ?

6 my Is train this

   _____ ?

7 Look and write. Yes, it is.   No, it isn't.

1 Is this your doll? — Yes, it is.

2 Is this your ball? — No, it isn't.

3 Is this your car? — ___, ___.

4 Is this your teddy? — ___, ___.

5 Is this your train? — ___, ___.

6 Is this your kite? — ___, ___.

Unit 2

3 My body

Regular plural nouns
Present simple of be (2)
Demonstratives

Plural -s

 **Finger** is singular. We use the singular form when we are talking about one thing or person.

Fingers is plural. We use the plural form when we are talking about more than one thing or person.

plural = singular + **s**

 one finger → eight finger**s**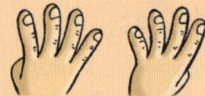

 one eye → two eye**s**

 one nose → four nose**s**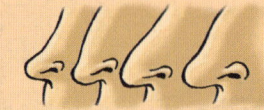

1 Complete the table.

Singular	Plural
arm	arms
ear	
	faces
leg	
	noses

16 Unit 3

2 Tick (✓) the correct one.

three finger ☐
three fingers ✓

one face ☐
one faces ☐

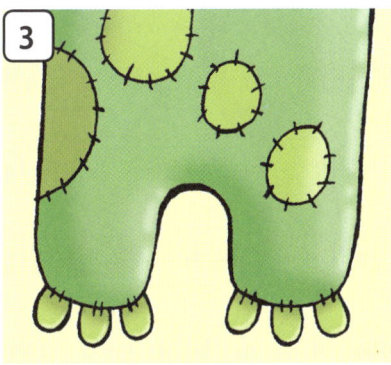

two legs ☐
two leg ☐

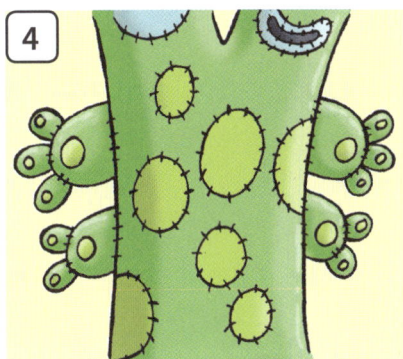

four arm ☐
four arms ☐

one hand ☐
one hands ☐

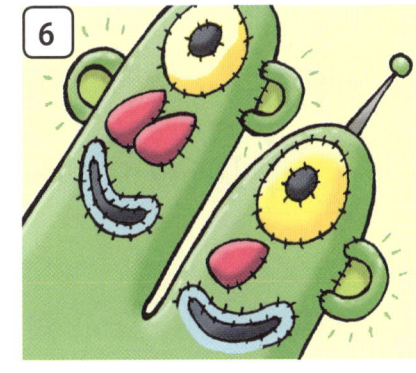

three ear ☐
three ears ☐

3 Count and write.

1 How many faces?
   _Two faces_____.

2 How many noses?
   _____.

3 How many ears?
   _____.

4 How many arms?
   _____.

5 How many fingers?
   _____.

6 How many eyes?
   _____.

Unit 3   17

Are

These **are** the faces! Yellow faces!

These **are** the eyes! Blue eyes!

These **are** the ears! Green ears!

We use **are** to identify things and people. **Are** comes from the verb **be**. Here **are** identifies two or more things or people.

These *are* eyes. The eyes *are* blue.

The nose *is* red.   The noses *are* red.

4 Match.

are

is

5 Write sentences. Use **is** or **are**.

1 legs / blue

   The legs are blue   .

2 nose / pink

   The _____.

3 arms / purple

   The _____.

4 fingers / green

   _____.

5 face / yellow

   _____.

Unit 3

This and these

This and **these** are demonstratives. We use them for things that are close to us.

Singular (one thing or person)
This is my kite.

Plural (two or more things or people)
These are my pencils.

6 Match.

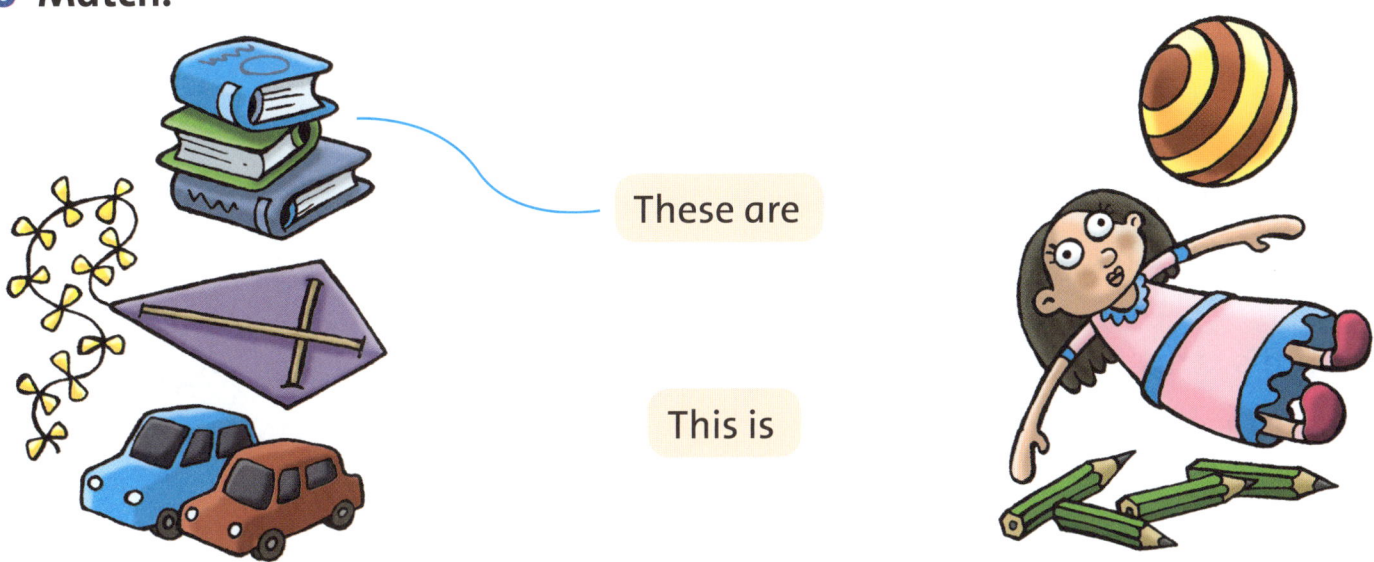

These are

This is

7 Write **This** or **These**.

1 _This_ is my ball.
2 _____ are my cars.
3 _____ are my trains.
4 _____ is my teddy.
5 _____ is my doll.
6 _____ are my puzzles.

Unit 3

Review 1

1 Write the words in the correct order. Then match.

1. What's your name?
2. Who's this?
3. How are you?
4. How old are you?
5. How many books?

is   Mary   This
<u>This is Mary</u>.

name's   My   Tom
_____.

six   I'm
_____.

books   Five
_____.

you   fine   I'm   thank
_____ fine, _____.

2 Write questions and answers.

rubber   pen   door   eye   arm   ~~ear~~

1. What's <u>this</u>?
   It's <u>an ear</u>.

2. What's <u>this</u>?
   It's _____.

3. _____?
   _____.

4. _____?
   _____.

5. _____?
   _____.

6. _____?
   _____.

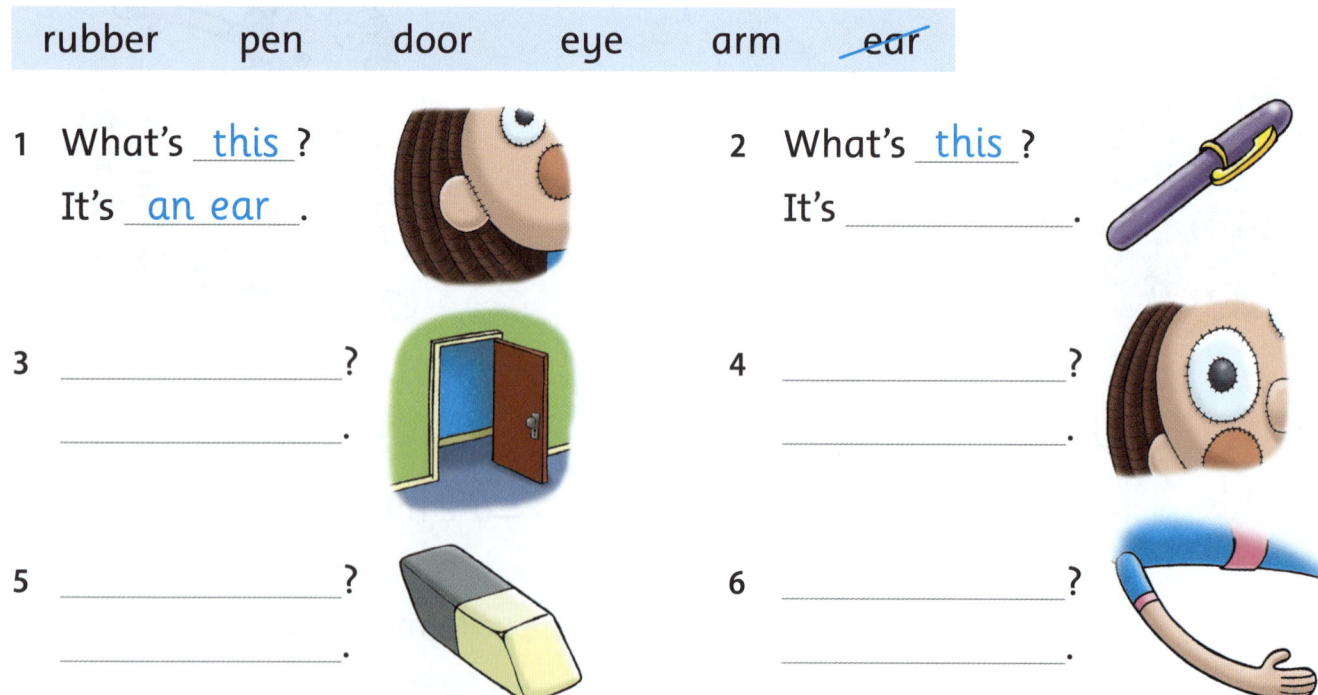

20   Review 1

3 Write the words in the correct box.

doll teddy pencils pens ball train car plane

my
doll
_____
_____
_____
_____

your
teddy
_____
_____
_____
_____

4 Write.

Yes, it is.   No, it isn't.

1 Is it a boy?
   No , it isn't .

2 Is it a window?
   _____ , _____ .

3 Is it a window?
   _____ , _____ .

4 Is it a girl?
   _____ , _____ .

5 Write **This is** or **These are**. Then match.

1 These are   my eyes.   b
2 _____ my ears.   ___
3 _____ my nose.   ___
4 _____ my face.   ___
5 _____ my arms.   ___

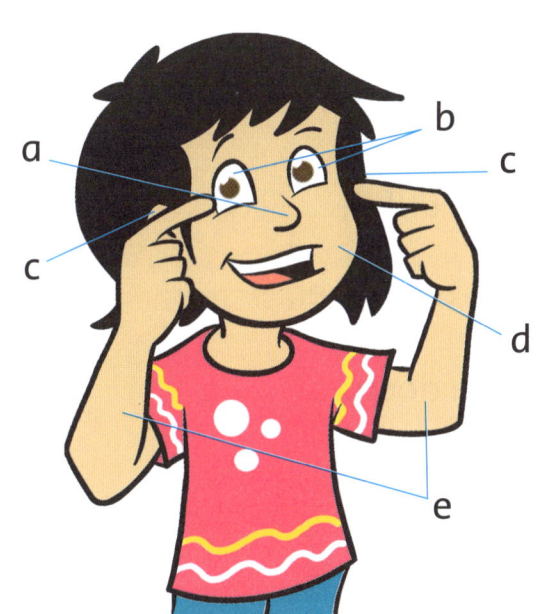

Review 1

4 Jobs

Subject pronouns (1)
Yes/no questions (1)

He and she

He and she are subject pronouns.

We use **he** when we talk about males (boys and men).

We use **she** when we talk about females (girls and women).

We use **it** when we talk about a thing or an object.

Other subject pronouns are: **I**, **you**, **we**, **they**

1 Match.

1 She's a nurse.   c
2 He's a pupil.   ___
3 She's a teacher.   ___
4 He's a doctor.   ___
5 He's a fireman.   ___
6 She's a vet.   ___

a
b
c
d
e
f

2 Tick (✓) the correct one.

This is Jamie. She's a pupil. ☐
This is Jamie. He's a pupil. ✓

This is Mrs Smith. She's a housewife. ☐
This is Mrs Smith. He's a housewife. ☐

This is Mr Rogers. He's a vet. ☐
This is Mr Rogers. She's a vet. ☐

This is Mr Smith. She's an astronaut. ☐
This is Mr Smith. He's an astronaut. ☐

3 Write **He's** or **She's**, and **a** or **an**.

_He's a_ policeman.

She's a doctor.

_____ pilot.

_____ housewife.

_____ vet.

_____ astronaut.

Questions with is

Is he ...? and **Is she ...?** are yes/no questions. We change the word order in questions.

He's a policeman.

Is he a policeman?

he's = he is

We can use short answers if the question begins **Is he ...?** or **Is she ...?**

Is she a nurse?
Yes, she is.

Is she a vet?
No, she isn't.

No, she isn't. = No, she is not.

4 Tick (✓) the correct short answer.

1  Is she a housewife?   Yes, she is. ✓
                                             No, she isn't. ☐

2  Is he a fireman?   Yes, he is. ☐
                                            No, he isn't. ☐

3  Is he a pilot?   Yes, he is. ☐
                                          No, he isn't. ☐

4  Is she a vet?   Yes, she is. ☐
                                         No, she isn't. ☐

5 Look and write.

Yes, he is.   No, he isn't.   Yes, she is.   No, she isn't.

Is she a doctor?
_No_, _she isn't_.

Is he a pilot?
____, _____.

Is he a vet?
____, _____.

Is she a nurse?
____, _____.

Is she a housewife?
____, _____.

Is he a doctor?
____, _____.

6 Write the words in the correct order.

1  | she | a | housewife | Is |  | she | Yes | is |

Is she a housewife ?   _Yes_ , _she is_ .

2 | a | he | Is | policeman |  | he | isn't | No |

Is he _____ ?   ____ , _____ .

3 | doctor | Is | a | she |  | isn't | No | she |

Is _____ ?   ____ , _____ .

4  | teacher | Is | a | she |  | is | she | Yes |

_____ ?   ____ , _____ .

5  | he | a | fireman | Is | | is | Yes | he |

_____ ?   ____ , _____ .

Unit 4   25

5 At the park

Wh- questions (1)
Prepositions of place

Where's ...?

Where's the bag?

It's on the swing.

Where's ...? is a wh- question. We can use it to ask about the place or position of something. We can reply with **It's ...**

We can also use **Where's ...?** to ask about the place or position of someone. Then we can reply with **He's ...** or **She's ...**

Where's ...? = Where is ...?

1 Look and write.

1  <u>Where's</u> the teddy?
<u>It's</u> in the bag.

2  _____ the bag?
_____ on the swing.

3 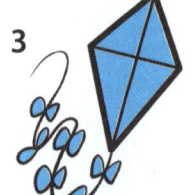 _____ ?
_____ under the slide.

4  _____ ?
_____ in the pool.

5  _____ Jamie?
_____ on the swing.

6  _____ Alison?
_____ under the slide.

26 Unit 5

In, on and **under**

The teddy is **in** the bag. The bag is **on** the swing. The kite is **under** the slide.

On, **in** and **under** are prepositions of place. They tell us where something or someone is.

2 Circle the prepositions in, on and under.

1
Where's the pencil?
It's (in) the pencil case.

2
Where's the doll?
It's under the seesaw.

3
Where's the bag?
It's on the swing.

4
Where's the ruler?
It's in the bag.

5
Where's the ball?
It's in the pool.

6
Where's the teddy?
It's under the slide.

Unit 5 27

3 Tick (✓) the correct sentence.

1 Where's the bag?   It's on the seesaw. ✓
It's under the seesaw. ☐
It's in the seesaw. ☐

2 Where's the doll?   It's in the bag. ☐
It's under the bag. ☐
It's on the bag. ☐

3 Where's the ball?   It's in the swing. ☐
It's on the swing. ☐
It's under the swing. ☐

4 Where's the teddy?   It's on the slide. ☐
It's under the slide. ☐
It's in the slide. ☐

5 Where's the kite?   It's on the swing. ☐
It's under the swing. ☐
It's in the swing. ☐

4 Read and draw the ball, the teddy, the car and the train.

1 The ball's in the pool.
2 The teddy's on the swing.
3 The car's under the slide.
4 The train's on the seesaw.

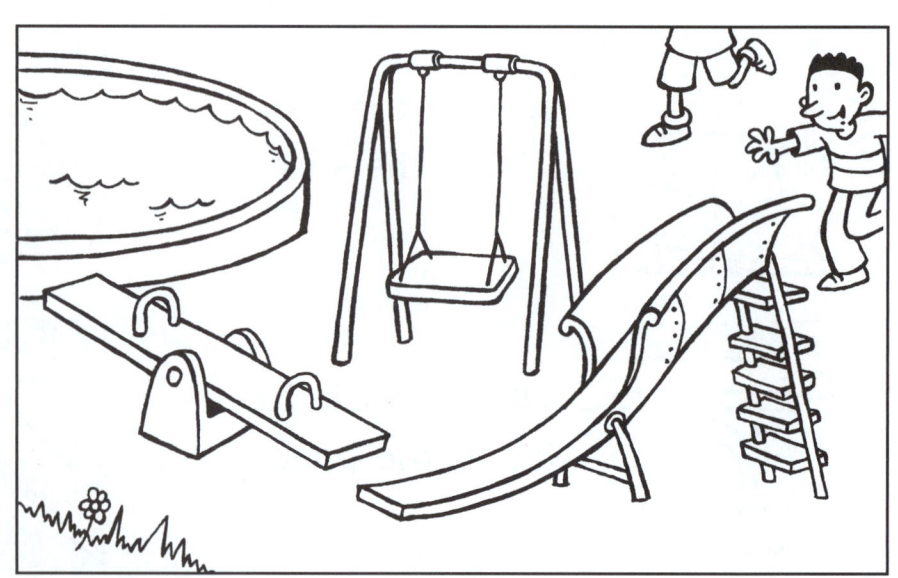

28   Unit 5

5 Look and write the questions.

1 Where's the teddy?
   It's in the pool.

2 _____?
   It's under the slide.

4 _____?
   It's under the swing.

5 _____?
   It's on the seesaw.

6 Look and write.

1 Where's the ball?
   It's under the swing.

2 _____ the teddy?
   It's _____ the bag.

3 _____ the train?
   _____ the seesaw.

4 _____ the doll?
   _____ the swing.

5 _____ the car?
   _____ the swing.

6 _____ the kite?
   _____ the slide.

6 My family

Subject pronouns (2)
Yes/no questions (2)
Possessive 's

I'm and you're

I and you are subject pronouns. We use I for ourselves. We use you for a person we are talking to. The pronouns are:

Singular	Plural
I, you, he, she, it	we, you, they

I'm = I am   you're = you are

1 Draw yourself and write.

30   Unit 6

2 Number the pictures.

1 I'm Grandpa. 2 I'm Alison. 3 I'm Grandma.
4 I'm Jamie. 5 I'm Mum. 6 I'm Dad.

3 Write the words in the correct order.

1 my grandpa You're

   <u>You're my grandpa</u>.

2 my grandma You're

   _____.

3 my sister You're

   _____.

4 You my aren't sister

   _____.

5 my You're mum

   _____.

6 mum You my aren't

   _____.

Unit 6 31

Are you ...?

Are you ...? is a yes/no question. We use it to find out about people.

We change the word order in questions.

You are my brother.
Are you my brother?

you're = you are

4 Look and write.

A<u>re</u> you my sister?

A_____ y_____ my grandma?

A_____ y_____ my grandpa?

_____ d_____?

_____ m_____?

Yes, _____ my mum!

5 Circle the possessive 's.

This is Alison('s) family. Jamie is Alison's brother. And Mrs Robinson is his mum. Alison's dad is Mr Robinson. Grandma's name is Catherine. Grandpa's name is Ernie.

6 Follow and write.

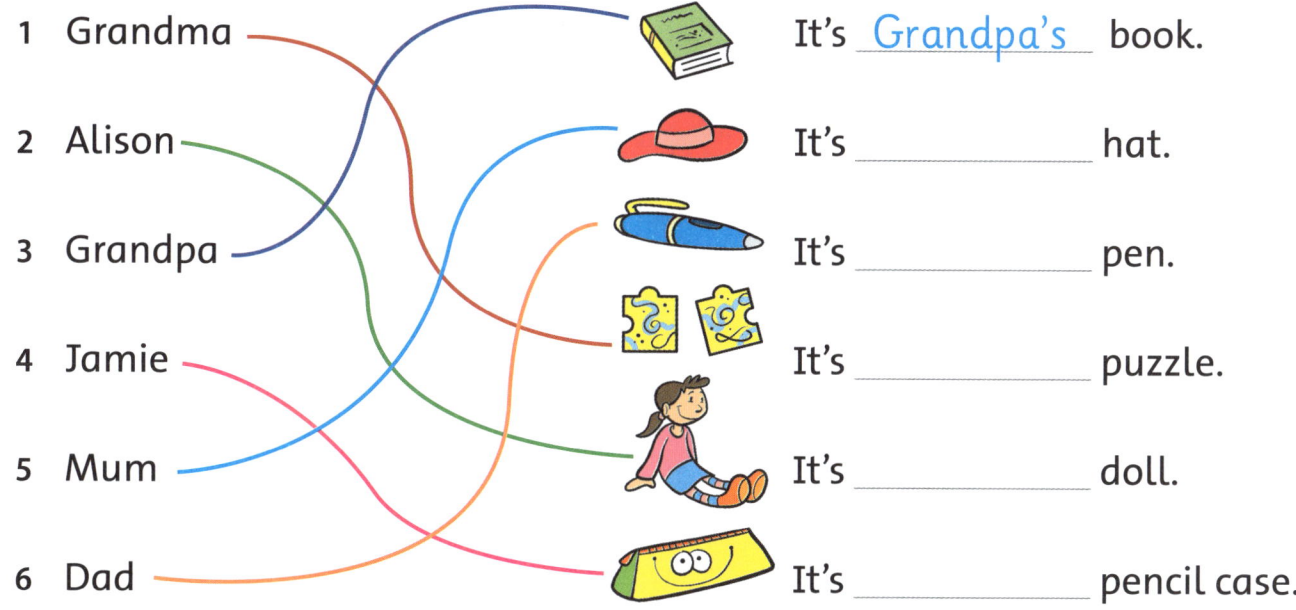

1 Grandma — It's _Grandpa's_ book.
2 Alison — It's _____ hat.
3 Grandpa — It's _____ pen.
4 Jamie — It's _____ puzzle.
5 Mum — It's _____ doll.
6 Dad — It's _____ pencil case.

Unit 6

Review 2

1 Write **She's a** or **He's a**.

1  __She's a__ vet.

2  _____ doctor.

3  _____ policeman.

4  _____ housewife.

5  _____ fireman.

6  _____ pilot.

2 Follow and write.

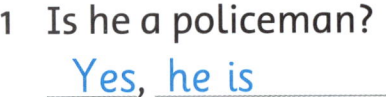

1 Is he a policeman?
   __Yes__, __he is__.

2 Is she a doctor?
   No, _____.

3 Is he a vet?
   Yes, _____.

4 Is she a housewife?
   _____, _____.

5 Is he a fireman?
   _____, _____.

6 Is she a pilot?
   _____, _____.

3 Write questions.

train   car   teddy   doll   ~~ball~~   kite

1 <u>Where's the ball</u> ?
   It's in the pool.

2 _____ ?
   It's on the swing.

3 _____ ?
   It's under the seesaw.

4 _____ ?
   It's in the tree.

5 _____ ?
   It's under the tree.

6 _____ ?
   It's in the bag.

4 Write.

Dad's   Mum's   Alison's   ~~Jamie's~~

1  <u>Jamie's</u> dad.

2  _____ mum.

3  _____ book.

4  _____ bag.

Review 2

7 Clothes

Yes/no questions (3)
Possessive adjectives (2)

Are they …? Yes, they are. No, they aren't.

Are they …? is a yes/no question. We can use it to ask about more than one person or thing.

Yes, they are and **No, they aren't** are short answers to the question **Are they …?**

Are they socks?   **Yes, they are.**   **Are they** trousers?   **No, they aren't.**

No, they aren't. = No, they are not.

1 Tick (✓) the correct short answer.

1 Are they shoes?
Yes, they are. ✓
No, they aren't. ☐

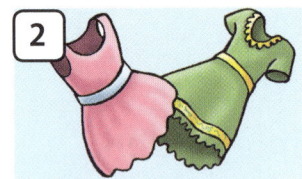

2 Are they dresses?
Yes, they are. ☐
No, they aren't. ☐

3 Are they coats?
Yes, they are. ☐
No, they aren't. ☐

4 Are they hats?
Yes, they are. ☐
No, they aren't. ☐

5 Are they T-shirts?
Yes, they are. ☐
No, they aren't. ☐

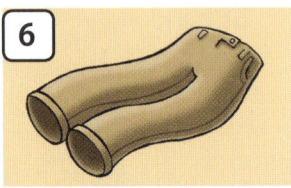

6 Are they socks?
Yes, they are. ☐
No, they aren't. ☐

2 Write.

Yes, they are.   No, they aren't.

1 Are they Mum's dresses?
   Yes , they are   .

2 Are they Dad's hats?
   No , they aren't   .

3 Are they Alison's socks?
   _____ , _____ .

4 Are they Dad's socks?
   _____ , _____ .

5 Are they Jamie's shoes?
   _____ , _____ .

6 Are they Mum's hats?
   _____ , _____ .

3 Look and write. Alison's or Jamie's?

Yes, it is.   No, it isn't.   Yes, they are.   No, they aren't.

1 Are they Jamie's shorts?
   Yes , they are   .

2 Are they Jamie's socks?
   _____ , _____ .

3 Is it Alison's hat?
   _____ , _____ .

4 Are they Jamie's shoes?
   _____ , _____ .

5 Is it Alison's T-shirt?
   _____ , _____ .

6 Is it Jamie's dress?
   _____ , _____ .

His and her

His and her are possessive adjectives. They say who owns something.

he (male)   **his** trousers, **his** shorts, **his** T-shirt
she (female)   **her** dress, **her** socks, **her** T-shirt

The other possessive adjectives are:

Pronoun	Possessive adjective
I	my
you	your
it	its
we	our
they	their

4 Match.

his

her

5 Write his or her.

 1 This is _his_ hat.
 2 This is _____ hat.

 3 This is _____ T-shirt.
 4 This is _____ T-shirt.

 5 This is _____ shoe.
 6 This is _____ shoe.

6 Write.

 1 They're Jamie's. They're his trousers.

 2 It's Alison's. It's her dress.

 3 _____. _____.

 4 _____. _____.

 5 _____. _____.

 6 _____. _____.

Unit 7

8 My home

Wh- questions (2)
Yes/no questions (4)
Adverbs

Where are ...?

 **Where are ...?** is a wh- question. We can use it to ask the place or location of more than one person or thing.
Where are Jamie and Dave?   **They're** in the garden.

We use **Where's ...?** to ask the place or location of one person or thing. (Where's ...? = Where is ...?)

1 Write Where's or Where are and the place.

1 __Where's__ Alison?
  She's in her __bedroom__.

2 _____ Jamie and Dave?
  They're in the _____.

3 _____ Mum?
  She's in the _____.

4 _____ Grandma and Grandpa?
  They're in the _____.

40   Unit 8

Is he in …? Is she in …? Are they in …?

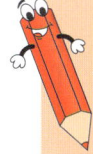 **Is she in …?** is a yes/no question. We can use it to ask if a person or thing is in the place we think.

Where's Alison? **Is she in** the living room?
Where's Jamie? **Is he in** the kitchen?
Where are Jamie and Dave? **Are they in** the hall?

2 Match.

   Are they in the hall?   Yes, he is.

   Is he in the living room?   Yes, they are.

   Are they in the kitchen?   No, he isn't.

   Is he in the bathroom?   No, they aren't.

3 Look and write.

> Is she   Is he   Are they   Yes, she is.   Yes, he is.
> No, he isn't.   No, she isn't.   Yes, they are.   No, they aren't.

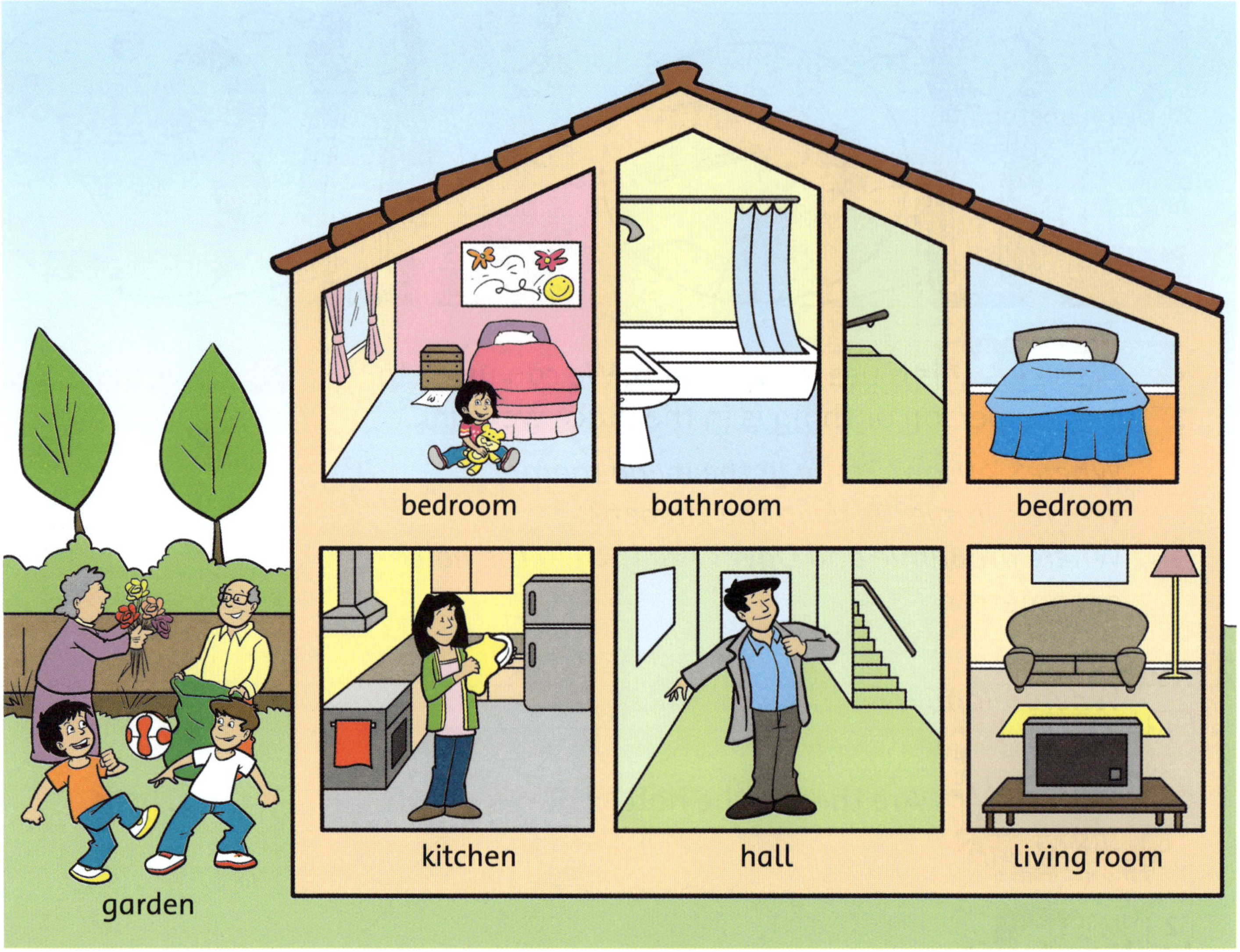

 1 <u>Are they</u> in the garden?
   <u>Yes</u> , <u>they are</u>   .

 2 _____ in the kitchen?
   ____ , _____ .

 3 _____ in the kitchen?
   ____ , _____ .

 4 _____ in the bedroom?
   ____ , _____ .

 5 _____ in the living room?
   ____ , _____ .

Unit 8

Upstairs and downstairs

upstairs

downstairs

Upstairs and downstairs are adverbs. They tell us where someone or something is in a house. Upstairs means at the top of the house. Downstairs means at the bottom of the house.

Where's Jamie?
He's **upstairs**.

Where's the bathroom?
It's **upstairs**.

Where are Alison and Mum?
They're **downstairs**.

Where are the kitchen and the dining room?
They're **downstairs**.

4 Look and write.

1 Where's Jamie?
He's _upstairs_.
He's _in the bathroom_.

2 Where are Alison and Mum?
They're _____.
They're _____.

3 Where's the kitchen?
It's _downstairs_.

4 Where's the bathroom?
_____.

5 Where's Dad?
_____.
_____.

6 Where's the hall?
_____.

Unit 8   43

9 My lunch

Have got (1)

I've got and **I haven't got**

 **I've got** says that you have or own something. **I haven't got** says that you don't have or own something.
I've got a sandwich. It's my sandwich.
I haven't got a banana.

I've got = I have got   I haven't got = I have not got

1 Alison or Jamie? Write A or J.

1 I've got a biscuit.   A
2 I've got two biscuits.   ___
3 I've got a banana.   ___
4 I haven't got a pear.   ___
5 I've got two pears.   ___
6 I've got a drink.   ___
7 I've got an apple.   ___
8 I haven't got an apple.   ___

44   Unit 9

2 Write the words in the correct order.

1. two   I've   got   sandwiches

   I've got two sandwiches.

2. two   got   I've   apples

   _____.

3. an   apple   haven't   I   got

   _____.

4. a   drink   got   I've

   _____.

5. egg   an   got   I've

   _____.

6. haven't   I   two   biscuits   got

   _____.

3 Look and write.

a drink   ~~a sandwich~~   an apple   a biscuit

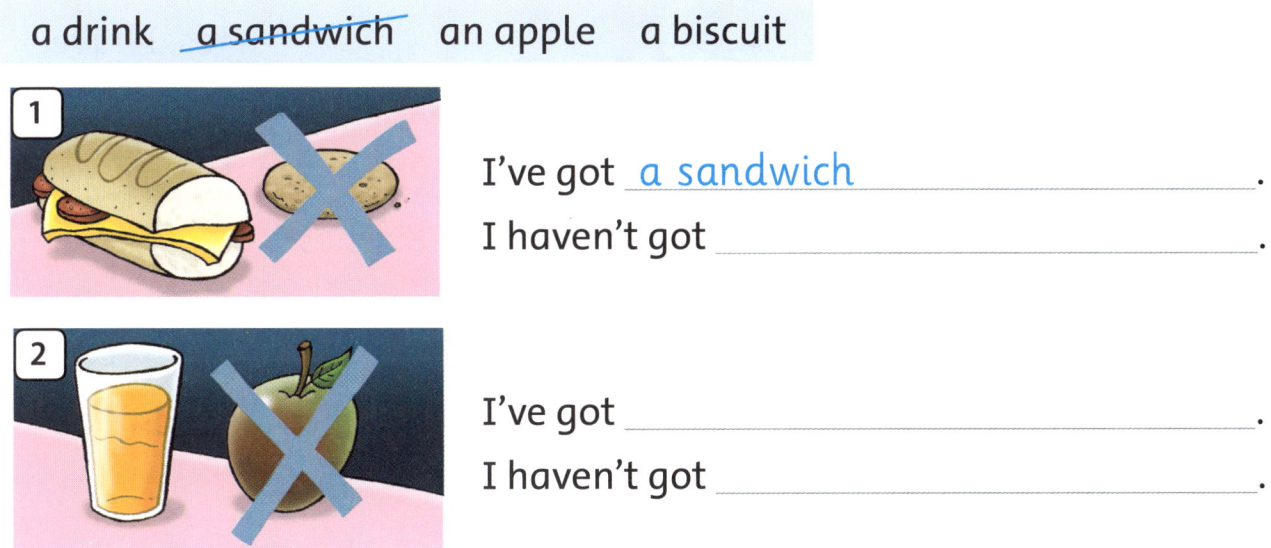

1. I've got a sandwich.
   I haven't got _____.

2. I've got _____.
   I haven't got _____.

Unit 9   45

Have you got ...? Yes, I have. No, I haven't.

Have you got ...? is a yes/no question. We can use it to ask about the things people have.

Yes, I have and **No, I haven't** are short answers. We can use them if the question begins **Have you got ...?**

No, I haven't. = No, I have not.

4 Match.

1 Have you got an orange? ✓ — No, I haven't.
2 Have you got your pencils? ✗ — Yes, I have.
3 Have you got a drink? ✓ — No, I haven't.
4 Have you got your sandwich? ✗ — Yes, I have.

5 Write the words in the correct order. Make questions.

1 got Have you a lunchbox

   <u>Have you got a lunchbox</u> ?

2 two sandwiches got Have you

   _____ ?

3 an egg got you Have

   _____ ?

4 you got a banana Have

   _____ ?

46 Unit 9

6 Look and write.

Yes, I have.   No, I haven't.

1 Have you got a banana?   Yes , I have   .
2 Have you got an egg?   ____ , _____.
3 Have you got a biscuit? ____ , _____.
4 Have you got a sandwich? ____ , _____.
5 Have you got a drink?   ____ , _____.
6 Have you got an apple?   ____ , _____.

7 Look and write.

Have you got?   Yes, I have.   No, I haven't.

1 Emma: Have you got a pear?   2 Jamie: _____ a biscuit?
  Jamie: Yes , I have   .   Dave: ____ , _____.

3 Emma: _____ a pear? 4 Dave: _____ a sandwich?
  Dave: ____ , _____.   Jamie: ____ , _____.

5 Jamie: _____ a sandwich? 6 Dave: _____ a pear?
  Emma: ____ , _____.   Emma: ____ , _____.

Unit 9   47

Review 3

1 Write **This is** or **These are** and **his** or **her**.

1  <u>This is his</u> hat.

2 _____ hat.

3 _____ trousers.

4 _____ shoes.

5 _____ shoes.

6 _____ dress.

7 _____ coat.

2 Write.

Yes, they are.   No, they aren't.

1  Are they her shoes?
<u>No</u> , <u>they aren't</u> .

2 Are they his socks?
_____ , _____.

3  Are they her shoes?
_____ , _____.

4 Are they his socks?
_____ , _____.

5  Are they her trousers?
_____ , _____.

6  Are they her dresses?
_____ , _____.

48 Review 3

3 Write **I've got** and a word from the box.

a sandwich   a drink   a pear   a sandwich   a tomato   an orange

1 I've got a sandwich.
2 _____.
3 _____.

4 _____.
5 _____.
6 _____.

4 Look and write.

Yes, I have.   No, I haven't.

1 Have you got a tomato?   Yes , I have .
2 Have you got a sandwich?   ____ , _____ .
3 Have you got a pear?   ____ , _____ .
4 Have you got a sandwich?   ____ , _____ .
5 Have you got a drink?   ____ , _____ .
6 Have you got an orange?   ____ , _____ .

Review 3   49

10 My friends

Have got (2)

He's got, she's got and it's got

This is Jamie. He's got short hair. He's got brown eyes.

This is Jamie's friend. Her name's Angie. She hasn't got short hair. She's got long hair. She's got green eyes.

He's got, she's got and **it's got** say that a person or thing has or owns something.

She's got a doll. It's her doll.

We also use them to say how people and things look.

Affirmative	Negative
He's got short hair.	**He hasn't got** long hair.
It's got four sides.	**It hasn't got** four sides.

…'s got = has got   … hasn't got = has not got

1 Read and circle.

1  (**It's**) / She's / He's got four legs.

2  **It** / **She** / **He** hasn't got long hair.

3  **It's** / **She's** / **He's** got three sides.

4  **It's** / **She's** / **He's** got a ball.

5  **It's** / **She's** / **He's** got a hat.

6  **It** / **She** / **He** hasn't got a hat.

2 Look, read and write the names.

1. She's got long hair.
   Angie
2. He's got a puzzle.
   Billy
3. She's got a white dress.
   _____
4. He's got a book.
   _____
5. She's got a bag.
   _____
6. He's got a white T-shirt.
   _____
7. She's got black hair.
   _____
8. She's got brown hair.
   _____

3 Write the words in the correct order.

1.

He's   a   got   biscuit

He's got a biscuit_____.

2.

three   got   It's   sides

It's _____.

3.

black   hair   got   She   hasn't

_____.

4.

bike   a   He's   got

_____.

Unit 10

4 Look and write. Use **He's got** or **She's got** and words from the box.

| ~~short hair~~ | grey trousers | a lunchbox | a blue T-shirt |
| ~~long hair~~ | a blue hat | a yellow T-shirt | a bag |

1 <u>He's got short hair</u>.
2 _____.
3 _____.
4 _____.

5 <u>She's got long hair</u>.
6 _____.
7 _____.
8 _____.

5 Look and write. Use **It's got** and words from the box.

| long | short | triangle | rectangle | ~~square~~ |

1

What's this?
<u>It's got</u> four sides. It's a <u>square</u>.

2

What's this?
_____ two _____ sides and one _____ side. It's a _____.

3

What's this?
_____ two _____ sides and two _____ sides. It's a _____.

6 Make the sentences negative.

1 He's got long hair. <u>He hasn't got long hair</u>.
2 She's got black hair. _____.
3 It's got big eyes. _____.
4 She's got green socks. _____.
5 He's got black trousers. _____.

7 Look and write.

| He's got | She's got | It's got | He hasn't got | She hasn't got | It hasn't got |

	puzzle	doll	ball
Jamie	✓	✗	✓
Angie	✗	✓	✗
Dave	✓	✗	✗
cat	✗	✗	✓

Jamie
1 <u>He's got a puzzle</u>.
2 <u>He hasn't got a doll</u>.
3 <u>He's got a ball</u>.

Angie
4 _____.
5 _____.
6 _____.

Dave
7 _____.
8 _____.
9 _____.

The cat
10 _____.
11 _____.
12 _____.

Unit 10   53

11 Zoo trip

Present simple: *like* (1)
Adjectives

I like and **I don't like**

I like and **I don't like** are present simple forms of the verb **like**. We use the present simple to talk about things that are true now.

Affirmative
☺ **I like**

Negative
☹ **I don't like**

don't = do not

1 Match.

2 Write **I like** or **I don't like**.

1. _I like_ giraffes.
2. _____ monkeys.
3. _____ snakes.

4. _____ tigers.

3 Look and write.

	🐘	🐍	🐒
Alison	🙂	☹️	🙂
Jamie	☹️	☹️	🙂
Mum	🙂	🙂	🙂
Dad	🙂	☹️	☹️

Like: 🙂   Don't like: ☹️

1 Alison: _I like_ elephants. _I don't like_ snakes. _I like_ monkeys.

2 Jamie: _____ elephants. _____ snakes. _____ monkeys.

3 Mum: _____ elephants. _____ snakes. _____ monkeys.

4 Dad: _____ elephants. _____ snakes. _____ monkeys.

4 What do you like? Then write about you.

1 _I like zebras_.   2 _____.
3 _____.   4 _____.
5 _____.   6 _____.

Unit 11

Adjectives

 **Green** and **tall** are adjectives. Adjectives describe things and people. Adjectives stay the same.

 It's **big**.   They're **big**.

5 Match.

1. It's tall.   b
2. It's short.   ___
3. They're big.   ___
4. They're long. ___
5. They're little. ___
6. It's orange.   ___

6 Write.

~~big~~   little   ~~blue~~   red   long   yellow   short   tall   green

1. It's big .
2. They're blue .
3. _____ .

4. _____ .
5. _____ .
6. _____ .

7. _____ .
8. _____ .
9. _____ .

7 Circle the adjectives. True or false? Write T or F.

1. Elephants are (green).   F
2. Giraffes are short.   ___
3. Elephants are big.   ___
4. Snakes are tall.   ___
5. Frogs are little.   ___

Unit 11   57

12 Family meal

Present simple: *like* (2)
Wh- questions (3)

Do you like ...?

Do you like ...? is a yes/no question. The short answers are **Yes, I do** or **No, I don't**. It is the present simple interrogative form.

Do you like + 🍎🍎 + ? = **Do you like apples?** **Yes, I do.**

Do you like + 🍌 + ? = **Do you like bananas?** **No, I don't.**

1 Write the words in the correct order. Make questions.

1. you Do like meat — <u>Do you like meat</u>?
2. like Do oranges you — Do you _____?
3. like bread Do you — Do _____?
4. rice like you Do — _____?
5. like Do tomatoes you — _____?
6. you like fish Do — _____?

2 Write questions.

1. bread — Do you like bread ?
2. carrots — Do you _____ ?
3. bananas — _____ ?
4. rice — _____ ?

3 Match.

1 Do you like fish? ☹
2 Do you like meat? ☺
3 Do you like carrots? ☹
4 Do you like apples? ☺
5 Do you like rice? ☺
6 Do you like bread? ☹

Yes, I do.

No, I don't.

4 Write.

Yes, I do.   No, I don't.

1 Do you like meat?   ☺ Yes , I do .
2 Do you like carrots? ☹ _____ , _____ .
3 Do you like fish?   ☹ _____ , _____ .
4 Do you like bread?   ☺ _____ , _____ .
5 Do you like juice?   ☺ _____ , _____ .
6 Do you like milk?   ☹ _____ , _____ .

Unit 12 59

What do you like?

What do you like? is a wh- question.
We can reply:
☺ **I like** yogurt.   ☹ **I don't like** fish.

5 Write the words in the correct order.

1. do   What   like   you

   <u>What do you like</u> ?

2. you   Do   like   bananas

   _____ ?

3. you   Do   fish   like

   _____ ?

4. you   like   do   What

   _____ ?

5. like   I   bread

   _____ .

6. don't   I   like   bread

   _____ .

7. like   What   you   do

   _____ ?

8. carrots   I   like   don't

   _____ .

60   Unit 12

6 Look and write.

1. Jamie: __What do you like__, Emma?
2. Emma: __I like fish__.
3. Emma: __Do you like fish__, Jamie?
4. Jamie: __Yes__, __I do__.

5. Angie: __What do you like__, Dave?
6. Dave: _____.
7. Dave: _____, Angie?
8. Angie: _____.

9. Emma: _____, Angie?
10. Angie: _____.
11. Angie: _____, Emma?
12. Emma: _____.

Unit 12

Review 4

1 Write **She's got** or **She hasn't got**.

1. _She's got_ long hair.
2. _She hasn't got_ short hair.
3. _____ straight hair.
4. _____ curly hair.
5. _____ black hair.
6. _____ brown hair.
7. _____ a doll.
8. _____ a teddy.

2 Write the words in the correct order.

1. like I lions

   I like lions .

2. monkeys like I

   _____ .

3. don't I elephants like

   _____ .

4. don't like I snakes

   _____ .

5. giraffes like I

   _____ .

6. I like don't monkeys

   _____ .

3 Match.

1. It's big.   _c_
2. They're long. ___
3. They're tall. ___
4. It's long.   ___
5. It's small.   ___
6. It's short.   ___

a  b  c

d  e  f

4 Write.

No, I don't. Yes, I do.

1. Mum: Do you like carrots?
   Ann: __No__ , __I don't.__ .

2. Mum: Do you like bread?
   Ann: _____ , _____ .

3. Mum: Do you like rice?
   Ann: _____ , _____ .

4. Mum: Do you like bananas?
   Ann: _____ , _____ .

5. Mum: Do you like apples?
   Ann: _____ , _____ .

6. Mum: Do you like yogurt?
   Ann: _____ , _____ .

5 Look and write.

What   ~~Do~~   No   like   don't   I

1. __Do__ you like tomatoes?
   _____ , I don't.

2. Do you _____ fish?
   No, I _____ .

3. _____ do you like?
   _____ like meat!

Review 4

13 My room

There's and *there are*

There's and There are

There are four rooms.
There's a bed.
There's a cupboard.

We use **there's** and **there are** to talk about things around us.

We use **there's** to talk about one thing or person.
There's a bed.   *There's* a cupboard.

We use **there are** to talk about two or more things or people.
There are four rooms.

there's = there is

1 Match.

1. There are two toy boxes. _e_
2. There's a toy box. ____
3. There's a doll. ____
4. There are three dolls. ____
5. There are four books. ____
6. There's a book. ____

2 Write the words in the correct box.

a bed   eight books   two pillows   a cupboard   five pencils
ten cars   a doll   six puzzles   a shelf   a blanket

There's

a bed

There are

eight books

3 Count. Write sentences.

1 There's one   teddy.
2 There are five   dolls.
3 _____ balls.
4 _____ puzzle.
5 _____ kite.
6 _____ books.
7 _____ bed.
8 _____ shelf.

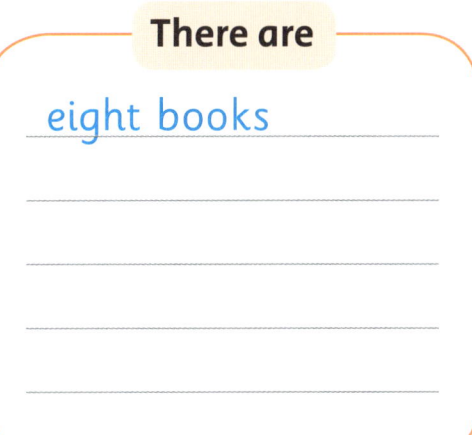

Unit 13 65

Is there …?

 **Is there …?** is a yes/no question. We can use **Is there …?** to ask about things around us.

We change the word order in questions.
There's a pillow on the bed.
Is there a pillow on the bed?

4 Write the words in the correct order. Make questions.

1 there Is a pillow

   Is there a pillow ?

2 there Is a toy box

   _____ ?

3 shelf a Is there

   _____ ?

4 a bed there Is

   _____ ?

5 a Is cupboard there

   _____ ?

6 rug Is a there

   _____ ?

66 Unit 13

Yes, there is. No, there isn't.

Is there a car? — **Yes, there is.**

Is there a train? — **No, there isn't.**

Yes, there is and **No, there isn't** are short answers. We can use them if the question begins **Is there ...?**

Is there a ball?
Yes, there is.
No, there isn't.

No, there isn't. = No, there is not.

5 Tick (✓) the correct short answer.

1. Is there a bed? — No, there isn't. ☐ / Yes, there is. ✓
2. Is there a shelf? — No, there isn't ☐ / Yes, there is. ☐
3. Is there a toy box? — No, there isn't. ☐ / Yes, there is. ☐
4. Is there a cupboard? — No, there isn't. ☐ / Yes, there is. ☐

6 Look and write.

Yes, there is.   No, there isn't.

1. Is there a car on the shelf?   __Yes__ , __there is__ .
2. Is there a ball on the shelf?   _____ , _____ .
3. Is there a blanket on the bed?   _____ , _____ .
4. Is there a cupboard?   _____ , _____ .

Unit 13

14 Abilities

Can for ability

Can and can't

Can means that you are able to do something. It always comes before another verb.
A bird **can** fly. It **can** fly.
Alison **can** run. She **can** run.

Can't means that you are not able to do something.
A snake **can't** run. It **can't** run.
Jamie **can't** fly. He **can't** fly.

can't = cannot

1 True or false? Write T or F.

 1. A bird can sing. __T__
A bird can't sing. __F__

 2. A monkey can sing. ____
A monkey can't sing. ____

 3. A fish can swim. ____
A fish can't swim. ____

 4. A parrot can swim. ____
A parrot can't swim. ____

 5. A snake can run. ____
A snake can't run. ____

 6. A tiger can run. ____
A tiger can't run. ____

2 Write the words in the correct order.

1  zebra A can't fly

A zebra can't fly.

2 A walk can't fish

_____.

3  monkey A can run

_____.

4 parrot A swim can't

_____.

5  A talk can't cat

_____.

6 can play Alison

_____.

3 Write **can** or **can't**.

1 Jamie _can_ write.
  A monkey _____ write.

2 Jamie _____ swim.
  A fish _____ swim.

3 Jamie _____ run.
  A snake _____ run.

4 A bird _____ fly.
  Jamie _____ fly.

4 Write true sentences.

	sing	run	climb	fly
bird	✓	✗	✗	✓
monkey	✗	✓	✓	✗

1 bird / sing
  A bird can sing.

2 monkey / fly
  A monkey can't fly.

3 bird / run
  _____.

4 monkey / climb
  _____.

5 bird / fly
  _____.

6 monkey / run
  _____.

7 bird / climb
  _____.

8 monkey / sing
  _____.

Unit 14

5 Tick (✓) and write about you.

	I can	I can't
talk	✓	
run		
fly		
walk		
sing		
swim		

1 I can talk.
2 _____.
3 _____.
4 _____.
5 _____.
6 _____.

Can it …?   Yes, it can.   No, it can't.

 **Can it …?** is a yes/no question. We use it to find out what animals and things are able to do.

Yes, it can and **No, it can't** are short answers. We can use them if the question begins **Can it …?**

Can it run?   ✓ Yes, it can.   ✗ No, it can't.

We use **can he** or **can she** to find out what people are able to do.

6 Match.

Can it fly?   Can it swim?   Can it climb?   Can it climb?   Can it run?   Can it run?

No, it can't.   Yes, it can.

7 Look and write.

| Can he | Can she | Can it | ~~Yes, he can~~ | Yes, he can |
| Yes, it can | No, she can't | No, she can't | No, it can't | |

1  Can he run?
   <u>Yes</u> , <u>he can</u> .

2  Can she swim?
   _____ , _____ .

3  Can it run?
   _____ , _____ .

4  _____ talk?
   _____ , _____ .

5  _____ fly?
   _____ , _____ .

6  _____ climb?
   _____ , _____ .

Unit 14

15 At the beach

Let's
Imperatives
Negative imperatives

Let's

Let's play football.

Let's run!

Let's make a sandcastle.
That's a good idea.

We use **let's** as a way of suggesting to somebody that you do something together. **Let's** always comes before another verb.

| Let's | walk.
run.
climb.
talk.
sing.
draw. | Let's | play football.
find shells.
swim in the sea.
go in a boat.
write.
make a sandcastle. |

let's = let us

1 Match.

1 Let's make a sandcastle.   d
2 Let's play football.   ___
3 Let's draw.   ___
4 Let's find shells.   ___
5 Let's go in a boat.   ___
6 Let's swim in the sea.   ___

a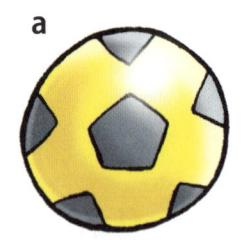

b

c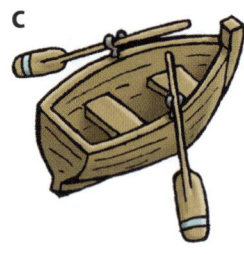

d

e

f

2 Look and write. Use **Let's** and the words in the box.

~~read~~   find shells   have an ice lolly   play football
make a sandcastle   swim in the sea

Jamie: Let's read _____.

Jamie: _____.

Jamie: _____.

Jamie: _____.

Jamie: _____.

Jamie: _____.

3 Write the words in the correct order.

1 swim in sea Let's the

   Let's swim in the sea.

2 football Let's play

   _____.

3 Let's a sandcastle make

   _____.

4 shells find Let's

   _____.

5 ice lolly an Let's have

   _____.

6 good idea That's a

   _____.

Imperatives

Jump and **run** are imperative forms. We can use an imperative to tell somebody to do something.

! This is an exclamation mark. We often use it at the end of the sentence when the verb is an imperative.

4 Match.

1. Find the ball!   _a_
2. Run!   ___
3. Catch the ball!   ___
4. Wait!   ___
5. Look!   ___

Negative imperatives

Don't forget your hat, Alison.

Don't forget is a negative imperative. We can use a negative imperative to tell somebody not to do something. We use **don't** and a verb.

Imperative	Negative imperative
Forget.	**Don't** forget.
Run.	**Don't** run.
Look.	**Don't** look.

don't = do not

5 Make the imperatives negative.

1 Walk!   Don't walk !
2 Run!   _____!
3 Stand up!   _____!
4 Play ball!   _____!
5 Have an ice lolly!   _____!

6 Look and write.

Don't swim   Don't walk   Don't fly   Don't run

1 Don't run !

2 _____ a kite!

3 _____!

4 _____!

Unit 15

Review 5

1 Describe the picture.

1 There are _five T-shirts_____.
2 There's _____.
3 _____.
4 _____.
5 _____.
6 _____.

2 Match.

1 It can swim. _e_
2 She can't swim. ___
3 He can draw. ___
4 He can sing. ___
5 She can jump. ___
6 It can't jump. ___

76   Review 5

3 Write short answers.

1 Can it swim?
Yes , it can .

2 Can it talk?
_____ , _____ .

3 Can she swim?
_____ , _____ .

4 Can it climb?
_____ , _____ .

5 Can he draw?
_____ , _____ .

6 Can it sing?
_____ , _____ .

4 Look and write.

| Let's run | Let's swim | Let's go | Let's climb |

 1 Let's run !

 2 _____ !

 3 _____ !

 4 _____ in a boat!

5 Look and write.

| Don't walk | Don't swim | Fly | Draw |

 1 Don't swim !

 2 _____ a picture!

 3 _____ !

 4 _____ !

Grammar reference

Units 2, 4, 6, 7

Subject pronouns	Possessive adjectives
I	my
you	your
he	his
she	her
it	its
we	our
they	their

Units 1–8 Be

Affirmative

Short form	Long form
I'm	I **am**
you're	you **are**
he's	he **is**
she's	she **is**
it's	it **is**
we're	we **are**
you're	you **are**
they're	they **are**

Negative

Short form	Long form
I'm **not**	I **am** not
you **aren't**	you **are** not
he **isn't**	he **is** not
she **isn't**	she **is** not
it **isn't**	it **is** not
we **aren't**	we **are** not
you **aren't**	you **are** not
they **aren't**	they **are** not

Interrogative / Short answers

Interrogative	Short answers	
am I?	Yes, I **am**.	No, I'm **not**.
are you?	Yes, you **are**.	No, you **aren't**.
is he?	Yes, he **is**.	No, he **isn't**.
is she?	Yes, she **is**.	No, she **isn't**.
is it?	Yes, it **is**.	No, it **isn't**.
are we?	Yes, we **are**.	No, we **aren't**.
are you?	Yes, you **are**.	No, you **aren't**.
are they?	Yes, they **are**.	No, they **aren't**.

Units 9–10 — Have got

Affirmative

Short form	Long form
I've got	I have got
you've got	you have got
he's got	he has got
she's got	she has got
it's got	it has got
we've got	we have got
you've got	you have got
they've got	they have got

Negative

Short form	Long form
I haven't got	I have not got
you haven't got	you have not got
he hasn't got	he has not got
she hasn't got	she has not got
it hasn't got	it has not got
we haven't got	we have not got
you haven't got	you have not got
they haven't got	they have not got

Interrogative

have I got?
have you got?
has he got?
has she got?
has it got?
have we got?
have you got?
have they got?

Short answers

Yes, I have.	No, I haven't.
Yes, you have.	No, you haven't.
Yes, he has.	No, he hasn't.
Yes, she has.	No, she hasn't.
Yes, it has.	No, it hasn't.
Yes, we have.	No, we haven't.
Yes, you have.	No, you haven't.
Yes, they have.	No, they haven't.

Units 11–12 — Like

Affirmative	Negative Short form	Long form
I like	I don't like	I do not like
you like	you don't like	you do not like
he likes	he doesn't like	he does not like
she likes	she doesn't like	she does not like
it likes	it doesn't like	it does not like
we like	we don't like	we do not like
you like	you don't like	you do not like
they like	they don't like	they do not like

Interrogative

do I like?
do you like?
does he like?
does she like?
does it like?
do we like?
do you like?
do they like?

Short answers

Yes, I do.	No, I don't.
Yes, you do.	No, you don't.
Yes, he does.	No, he doesn't.
Yes, she does.	No, she doesn't.
Yes, it does.	No, it doesn't.
Yes, we do.	No, we don't.
Yes, you do.	No, you don't.
Yes, they do.	No, they don't.

Grammar reference

Unit 13 — There is and there are

Affirmative		Negative	
Short form	Long form	Short form	Long form
there's	there is	there isn't	there is not
—	there are	there aren't	there are not

Interrogative	Short answers	
is there?	Yes, there is.	No, there isn't.
are there?	Yes, there are.	No, there aren't.

Unit 14 — Can

Affirmative	Negative	
	Short form	Long form
I can	I can't	I cannot
you can	you can't	you cannot
he can	he can't	he cannot
she can	she can't	she cannot
it can	it can't	it cannot
we can	we can't	we cannot
you can	you can't	you cannot
they can	they can't	they cannot

Interrogative	Short answers	
can I?	Yes, I can.	No, I can't.
can you?	Yes, you can.	No, you can't.
can he?	Yes, he can.	No, he can't.
can she?	Yes, she can.	No, she can't.
can it?	Yes, it can.	No, it can't.
can we?	Yes, we can.	No, we can't.
can you?	Yes, you can.	No, you can't.
can they?	Yes, they can.	No, they can't.

Unit 15 — Imperatives

Affirmative	Negative
catch	don't catch
find	don't find
fly	don't fly
forget	don't forget
have	don't have
jump	don't jump
look	don't look
play	don't play
run	don't run
stand up	don't stand up
swim	don't swim
wait	don't wait
walk	don't walk